A LOCAL HABITATION

A Local Habitation

NORMAN NICHOLSON

FABER AND FABER
3 Queen Square
London

First published in 1972
by Faber and Faber Limited
3 Queen Square London WC1
First published in this edition 1973
Printed in Great Britain by
The Bowering Press Plymouth

ISBN 0 571 10425 8   *(hard bound edition)*
ISBN 0 571 09982 3   *(paper covers)*

© 1972 *by Norman Nicholson*

... and gives to airy nothing
A local habitation and a name.
A Midsummer Night's Dream

For
Delmar and José Banner

Acknowledgements

Acknowledgements are due to the editors of the following: *English*, *Chirimo* (Rhodesia), *The London Magazine*, *The Malahat Review* (Canada), *The New Statesman*, *Phoenix*, *Stand*, *The Times Literary Supplement*, *The Transatlantic Review*.

On the Closing of Millom Ironworks first appeared in a Christmas Supplement of the Poetry Book Society, issued in memory of John Hayward, while *Have You Been to London?* and *The Dumb Spirit* have been published as Poetry Posters by the Mid-Northumberland Arts Group.

The Author wishes to express his gratitude to the donor and selection committee of the Cholmondeley Award, and also to Northern Arts, a grant from which, in 1969, enabled him to devote time to the writing of these poems.

Contents

THE DUMB SPIRIT

Eyes see
The shine and smother
Of world and otherworld—
The dumb spirit
Stifles the breath.

Ears hear
Clamour and song
Flung off the fly-wheel of the straining year—
The dumb spirit
Knots up the tongue.

Hands feel
The braille of creatures'
Meeting and mesh—
The dumb spirit
Dams the flow of the flesh.

Cast out the dumb,
Lord.
Touch ears.
Let spittle un-numb the tongue.
Let there be no impediment on lung or larynx,
And let the breath
Speak plain again.

THE BOREHOLE

A huddle of iron jammy-cranes
Straddles the skear, shanks
Rusty from salt rains,
Or half-way up their barnacled flanks
In the flood tide. Paid-up pits
Lounge round the banks,
Turning out red pockets.
The cranking waders stand,
Necks down, bills grinding in their sockets,
Drilling the sand.
A steam-pipe whistles, the clanged iron bells;
Five hundred feet of limestone shudders and
Creaks down all its strata'd spine of ammonites and shells
And a vertical worm of stone is worried
Out from the earth's core.
The daylight falls
Westward with the ebb, before
The night-shift buzzer calls:
But what is it sticks in the bird's gullet—
Rubble or crystal, dross or ore?

Jammy-cranes: herons.
Skear: a bank of shingle or stones exposed at low tide.

14

THE WHISPERER

For twenty months I whispered,
> Spoke aloud
> Not one word,
Except when the doctor, checking my chest, said:
> 'Say Ninety-nine',
> And, from the mine
Of my throat, hauling up my voice like a load of metal, I
> Said 'Ninety-nine.'
> From sixteen-
years-old to my eighteenth birthday I whispered clock
> And season round;
> Made no sound
More than the wind that entered without knocking
> Through the door
> That wasn't there
Or the slid-wide window that un-shuttered half the wall of my
> Shepherd's bothy
> Of a chalet.
In the hushed sanatorium night I coughed in whispers
> To stray cats
> And dogs that
Stalked in from the forest fogs to the warmth of my anthracite
> stove,
> And at first light
> Of shrill July
To the robin winding its watch beside spread trays of cedars.
> Day after day
> My larynx lay

In dry dock until whispering seemed
> The normal way
> Of speaking: I
Was surprised at the surprise on the face of strangers
> Who wondered why
> I was so shy.
When I talked to next-bed neighbours, out-of-breath on the
> Gravel track,
> They whispered back
As if the practice were infectious. Garrulous as a budgie,
> I filled the air
> Of my square
Thermometered and Lysolled cage with the agitated
> Wheezes, squeaks
> And wind-leaks
Of my punctured Northumbrian pipes. And when the doctor
> asked me
> How I felt, 'I'm
> Feeling fine',
I whispered—my temperature down to thirty-seven,
> The sore grate
> Soothed from my throat,
And all the winds of Hampshire to ventilate my lungs.

Two winters went whispered away before I ventured
> Out of my cage,
> Over the hedge,
On to the chalky chines, the sparse, pony-trodden, adder-
> ridden
> Grass. Alone
> Among pine

Trunks I whispered comfortable sermons to
            Congregations
            Of worms. Patients
On exercise in copse or on common, sighting me
            At distance, gave
            Me a wave,
And I in reply blew a blast on my police-
            man's whistle,
            Meaning: 'Listen.
Wait! Come closer. I've something to tell.'
            But when tea-
            time brought me
To drawing-room and chatter, the thunder of shook cups,
            Crack of laughter,
            Stunned and baffled
Me. I bawled in whispers four-inch from the ear
            Of him or her
            Unheeded. Words,
Always unheard, failed even articulate me.
            Frantic, I'd rap
            Table or clap
Hands, crying: 'Listen, for God's sake listen!' And suddenly
            the room
            Fell silent,
            Waiting, and I
Words failing again, fell silent too.
                              The world moved
            Noisily on.
            My larynx soon
Was afloat again but my life still drifts in whispers.
            I shout out loud
            To no crowd,

17

Straining to be heard above its strangling murmur, but
        Look for one face
        Lit with the grace
Of listening, the undeadened brow that marks an undeafened
        Ear. I try
        To catch an eye;
Nod, nudge, wink, beckon, signal with clicked
        Fingers, roll
        Words to a ball
And toss them for the wind to play with. Life roars round me
        like
        A dynamo.
        I stump, stamp, blow
Whistle over and over, staring into the rowdy air, seeking
        You or you,
        Anyone who
Can lip-read the words of my whisper as clear as the clang of a
        bell,
        Can see me say:
        'Wait! Wait!
        Come closer;
        I've something to tell.'

THE BLACK GUILLEMOT

Midway between Fleswick and St Bees North Head,
The sun in the west,
All Galloway adrift on the horizon;
The sandstone red
As dogwood; sea-pink, sea campion and the sea itself
Flowering in clefts of the cliff—
And down on one shelf,
Dozen on dozen pressed side by side together,
White breast by breast,
Beaks to the rock and tails to the fish-stocked sea,
The guillemots rest

Restlessly. Now and then,
One shifts, clicks free of the cliff,
Wings whirling like an electric fan—
Silhouette dark from above, with under-belly gleaming
White as it banks at the turn—
Dives, scoops, skims the water,
Then, with all Cumberland to go at, homes
To the packed slum again,
The rock iced with droppings.

I swing my binoculars into the veer of the wind,
Sight, now, fifty yards from shore,
That rarer auk: all black,
But for two white patches where the wings join the back,
Alone like an off-course migrant
(Not a bird of his kind
Nesting to the south of him in England),

Yet self-subsistent as an Eskimo,
Taking the huff if so much as a feather
Lets on his pool and blow-hole
In the floating pack-ice of gulls.

But, turn the page of the weather,
Let the moon haul up the tides and the pressure-hose of spray
Swill down the lighthouse lantern—then,
When boats keep warm in harbour and bird-watchers in bed,
When the tumble-home of the North Head's rusty hull
Takes the full heave of the storm,
The hundred white and the one black flock
Back to the same rock.

BOO TO A GOOSE

'You couldn't say *Boo* to a goose', my grandmother said
When I skittered howling in from the back street—my head
With a bump the size of a conker from a stick that someone
   threw,
Or my eyes rubbed red
From fists stuffed in to plug the blubbing. 'Not *Boo* to a goose,'
   she said,
But coddled me into the kitchen, gave me bread
Spread with brown sugar—her forehead,
Beneath a slashed, ash-grey bark of hair,
Puckered in puzzle at this old-fashioned child
Bright enough at eight to read the ears off
His five unlettered uncles, yet afraid
Of every giggling breeze that blew.
'There's nowt to be scared about,' she said,
'A big lad like you!'

But not as big as a goose—
                              or not the geese I knew,
Free-walkers of Slagbank Green.
From morning-lesson bell to supper-time
They claimed lop-sided common-rights between
Tag-ends of sawn-off, two-up-two-down streets
And the creeping screes of slag.
They plucked their acres clean
Of all but barley-grass and mud. Domesticated but never
   tamed,
They peeked down on you from their high
Spiked periscopes. No dog would sniff within a hundred yards

Of their wing-menaced ground.
At the first sound
Of a bicycle ring they'd tighten ranks,
Necks angled like bayonets, throttles sizzling,
And skein for the bare knees and the cranking shanks.
They were guarded like Crown Jewels. If any man were seen
To point a finger to a feather
He'd end up with boot-leather for his dinner.
They harried girls in dreams—and my lean
Spinning-wheel legs were whittled even thinner
From trundling round the green's extremest hem
To keep wide of their way.
No use daring me to say
Boo to them.

The girls grew up and the streets fell down;
Gravel and green went under the slag; the town
Was eroded into the past. But half a century later
Three geese—two wild, streaked brown-grey-brown
As the bog-cottoned peat, and one white farm-yard fly-off—
Held sentry astride a Shetland lochan. The crumbled granite
Tumbled down brae and voe-side to the tide's
Constricted entry; the red-throated diver jerked its clown-
striped neck, ducked, disappeared and perked up from the
    water
A fly-cast further on. The three geese took no notice.
But the moment I stepped from the hide of the car
The white one stiffened, swivelled, lowered its trajectory,
And threatened towards me. Then,
Under the outer arctic's summer arc of blue,
With a quick blink that blacked out fifty years
And a forgotten fear repeating in my stomach,

I found myself staring, level-along and through,
The eyes of that same slagbank braggart
I couldn't say *Boo* to.

THE ELVERS

An iron pipe
Syphoning gallons of brine
From the hundred foot below sea-level mine—
A spring salty as mussels,
Bilberry-stained with ore;
And the pink, dry-paper thrift rustles
In the draught made by the spray
As the pumps thrust the water upward
To a rock-locked bay.

And, quick in the brown burn,
Black whips that flick and shake,
Live darning-needles with big-eye heads—
Five-inch elvers
That for twice five seasons snake
Through the earth's turn and return of water
To seep with the swell into rifts of the old workings
And be churned out here on cinder beds and fern.

The pumps pour on.
The elvers shimmy in the weed. And I,
Beneath my parochial complement of sky,
Plot their way
From Sargasso Sea to Cumberland,
From tide to pit,
Knowing the why of it
No more than they.

BEE ORCHID AT HODBARROW

A hundred years ago
The swash channel
Filled at high water
And swilled dry
In runnels of sand at low—
Under the lea
Of the limestone shore,
Mine-shaft and funnel,
And the old light-house
On its stack of rejected ore.

Fifty years ago
The new sea-wall
Cordon'd and claimed
A parish no-one wanted,
A Jordan Valley without the Jordan,
Neither sea nor land,
Lower than low
Ebb-mark, arid
As wrack left lifted
High on the sand.

Only a backwash
Of rain drained inward
To a sumpy hollow
Above the old drifts—
Subsided tunnels
Open to the sky,
To rabbit and plover,

Neither submarine
Nor dry-land level,
Neither under nor over.

But now on the bare
Pate of the ground
See the bee orchid—
Neither plant nor animal,
A metaphysical
Conceit of a flower—
Heading the queue there,
First come, first served,
Where even ragwort's rare.

Decoy queens,
Honeyed and furred,
Linger and cling
To each lolling lobe;
Nervous, green-veined,
Lilac sepals
Prick at the twitch
Of a pollenating wing.

And stiff as a quill
In the splash of the grasses,
The whole articulated
Body of the flower—
Bloom, stem and leaf—
Is tense with need
To breed, to seed,
To colonize the new-found,
New-sunk island,

To snatch the brief
Between-tide hour
Of this limestone summer,
Before the sea
Pours in again
In three or four
Hundred years' time.

HODBARROW FLOODED

Where once the bogies bounced along hummocking tracks,
A new lake spreads its edges.
Where quarried ledges were loaded with red-mould ore,
Old winding towers
Up-ended float on glass.
Where once the shafts struck down through yielding limestone,
Black coot and moorhen
Lay snail-wakes on the water.

At seventy fathom
My Uncle Jack was killed
With half a ton of haematite spilled on his back.
They wound him up to the light
Still gasping for air.

Not even the rats can gasp there now:
For, beneath the greening spoil of a town's life-time,
The sixty, seventy,
Ninety fathom levels
Are long pipes and throttles of unflowing water,
Stifled cavities,
Lungs of a drowned man.

THE RIDDLE

Why is a baby
Like a railway engine?—I
Knew the answer, maybe
Forty years ago:
The night old Rustyknob
Of the jerry-laid iron mine,
All duck-waddle and puff,
Dived like a gannet,
Stream-feathered and slender,
Plumb in the deeps of the mine.
And the sand closed like water
Over piston-rod and spoke
Leaving not even the tender
Behind for a schoolboy's joke.

We stood in the steaming
November air
Staring at rails
Bent to no junction;
And switch-point levers
Left without function
Swivelled eyes wide
Down tracks of drifting shales—
And the son of the day-shift engine driver
Stood by my side.

The sand's slow tide
Flowed in and filled the crater;
Salted sleeper and chair.

Bolt and signal wire
Reddened like raspberries
In the soggy sea-air.
Thrift and sea-holly
Spilled on the dolly-tub rim,
Trefoil and clover
Yellowed it over,
Till not a dip the depth of a saucer
Scored the spot where the night-shift driver
Fought and fell clear,
And the bumpers bored down
To an underground siding,
Hauling a thousand brown
Bogey-loads of ore.

The dune-fly dances
In the jittery sun,
And skewers of marram
Peg down the ground-sheet sand.
But why is a baby?—
I forgot the answer
That muggy November
All Souls' Eve,
The night the engine died,
And only the old remember now,
And only the young believe.

WINDSCALE

The toadstool towers infest the shore:
Stink-horns that propagate and spore
    Wherever the wind blows.
Scafell looks down from the bracken band,
And sees hell in a grain of sand,
    And feels the canker itch between his toes.

This is a land where dirt is clean,
And poison pasture, quick and green,
    And storm sky, bright and bare;
Where sewers flow with milk, and meat
Is carved up for the fire to eat,
    And children suffocate in God's fresh air.

THE ELM DECLINE

The crags crash to the tarn; slow-
motion corrosion of scree.
From scooped corries,
bare as slag,
black sykes ooze
through quarries of broken boulders.
The sump of the tarn
slumps into its mosses—bog
asphodel, sundew, sedges—
a perpetual
sour October
yellowing the moor.

                  Seven
thousand years ago
trees grew
high as this tarn. The pikes
were stacks and skerries
spiking the green,
the tidal surge
of oak, birch, elm,
ebbing to ochre
and the wrackwood of backend.

                      Then
round the year Three
Thousand B.C.,
the proportion of elm pollen
preserved in peat

declined from twenty
per cent to four.

         Stone axes,
chipped clean from the crag-face,
ripped the hide off the fells.
Spade and plough
scriated the bared flesh,
skewered down to the bone.
The rake flaked into fragments
and kettlehole tarns
were shovelled chock-full
of a rubble of rotting rocks.

               Today

electric landslips
crack the rock;
drills tunnel it;
valleys go under the tap.
Dynamited runnels
channel a poisoned rain,
and the fractured ledges
are scoured and emery'd
by wind-to-wind rubbings
of nuclear dust.

         Soon
the pikes, the old
bottlestops of lava,
will stand scraped bare,
nothing but air round stone
and stone in air,

33

ground-down stumps
of a skeleton jaw—

                    Until
under the scree,
under the riddled rake,
beside the outflow of the reedless lake,
no human eye remains to see
a land-scape man
helped nature make.

SCREE

A million centuries it grew like a great tree
      Under the sea,
The wrack-ringed rock, lifting its branches higher
      Than the fire
Of black volcanoes burning in the green water. Coal
      Sprang from its bole
Like a parasitic plant; surf and sand
      Salted and
Silted it. Yet still the blunt trunk thrust
      Out through the crust
Shedding the paleozoic years like bark,
      While habitual, dark
Roots hankered back to unfossiliferous blocks
      Of rocks that made the rocks.
The wind rips off the wrap of sand till the tree stands bare
      In the hacksawing air,
Or under the rub of water, seep and sump,
      Worn to a stump,
Flakes away rind in a mildew of mist.
      Green-winged frost
With a woodpecker's prod and point
      Gimlets each joint;
Witch's broom, oak-apple, fungus, gall,
      Canker all
The crackles of the cork. A drool
      Of wood-rot and toadstool
Oozes from crevices, squirrel- and mouse-
      hole and tom-tit's house
Down to the ant-hill roots.

               The tree
        Disintegrates.

                    Scree
Is the autumn fall of the deciduous rock;
             Acorn-grey Oc-
tober of stone; compost of loam and lime;
            Cold leaf-mould of time.
Prolific as bacteria the one-cell seconds breed,
             Corrupting wall and weed,
                Depositing new seed.

SEPTEMBER ON THE MOSSES

Wait, tide, wait;
Let the mosses slide
In runnels and counter-flow of rock-pool green,
Where web-foot mud-weeds preen
Leaves spread in the sunshine; where
On slow air-ripples the marsh aster lays
Innocuous snare of sea-anemone rays.

Wait, tide, wait;
Behind your wide—
as-winter ebb the poplars of the waves
Turn up their underleaves of grey.
Thunder-blue shadows boom across the bay.
But here the silt is green, the salt is bright,
And every grass-tongue licks its summerful of light.

Autumnal tide,
Mauve as Michaelmas daisies, bide
Our while and summer's. Let the viscous sun
Percolate the turf. Let small becks run
Yellow for ever with shine, and the floor of this moment
Hold back time and shut the gate.
Wait, tide, wait.

Deciduous tide,
On the willow whips of inshore billows the inside
Edge is brown. Crying 'Never!'
Canutes no due tomorrow,
And now is ever

By being not by lasting. So
With pride let this long-as-life hour go,
And flow, tide, flow.

ONE MINUTE

To my Wife

Fifteen years ago—
The shut-down dark
Of hibernating February.
The park
Trees, ghosted in an underglow
Of lamp-wash, straining
Upwards to blackness;
Not even a star
To demonstrate by not being seen
The shape of the church-tower.
But spilled
On thefar
Cruck of the hill
The red-green rakings
Of the coke smoulder of day—
'Look!', you said,
Pointing to March,
The un-cocooning of a new year.

Fifteen more, and spring
Again unwinds itself;
Birds shout
In the thickening dusk.
The church-tower sprouts a pale
Blue steeple under the new moon;
The wickered willows
Still trellis the west;

Safe in the glowing grave-yard
Another generation is put to bed.
One minute tells the tale.—
And yet to make
Count of, find words for, all
These fifteen
Years add up to, mean
And span
('Yes!', you said,
Pointing to the small
Re-kindling of the dead end of day)
Could hardly take
That minute less than
Fifteen years.

AN ABSENCE OF ISLANDS

Look west
from Cumberland,
east from the North Sea shore,
where the wind is a spume of tossed terns and fulmars
or fumes with smothering feathers of soot;
look beyond seaweed and sewage,
pebbles and quick-sand and the oiled ebb channel—
and always,
at the far rim of the sea's grooved disk,
whatever the direction, whatever the slide of tide,
in an absence of islands
the horizon seems the same.

THE TUNE THE OLD COW DIED OF

'The tune the old cow died of,'
My grandmother used to say
When my uncle played the flute.
She hadn't seen a cow for many a day,
Shut in by slate
Walls that bound her
To scullery and yard and soot-
blackened flowerpots of hart's-tongue fern.
She watched her fourteen sons grow up around her
In a back street,
Blocked at one end by crags of slag,
Barred at the other by the railway goods-yard gate.
The toot of the flute
Piped to a parish where never cow could earn
Her keep—acres of brick
With telegraph poles and chimneys reared up thick
As ricks in a harvest field.
My grandmother remembered
Another landscape where the cattle
Waded half-way to the knees
In swish of buttercup and yellow rattle,
And un-shorn, parasite-tormented sheep
Flopped down like grey bolsters in the shade of trees,
And the only sound
Was the whine of a hound
In the out-of-hunting-season summer,
Or the cheep of wide-beaked, new-hatched starlings,
Or the humdrum hum of the bees.

Then

A cow meant milk, meant cheese, meant money,
And when a cow died
With foot-and-mouth or wandered out on the marshes
And drowned at the high tide,
The children went without whatever their father had promised.
When she was a girl
There was nothing funny,
My grandmother said,
About the death of a cow,
And it isn't funny now
To millions hungrier even than she was then.
So when the babies cried,
One after each for over fourteen years,
Or the flute squeaked at her ears,
Or the council fire-alarm let off a scream
Like steam out of a kettle and the whole mad town
Seemed fit to blow its lid off—she could find
No words to ease her mind
Like those remembered from her childhood fears:
'The tune the old cow died of.'

HAVE YOU BEEN TO LONDON?

'Have you been to London?'
My grandmother asked me.
                              'No.'—
China dogs on the mantelshelf,
Paper blinds at the window,
Three generations simmering on the bright black lead,
And a kettle filled to the neb,
Spilled over long ago.

I blew into the room, threw
My scholarship cap on the rack;
Wafted visitors up the flue
With the draught of my coming in—
Ready for Saturday's mint imperials,
Ready to read
The serial in *Titbits*, the evangelical
Tale in the parish magazine,
Under the green
Glare of the gas,
Under the stare of my grandmother's Queen.

My grandmother burnished her sleek steel hair—
Not a tooth in her jaw
Nor alphabet in her head,
Her spectacles lost before I was born,
Her lame leg stiff in the sofa corner,
Her wooden crutch at the steady:
'They shut doors after them
In London,' she said.

I crossed the hearth and thumped the door *to*;
Then turned to Saturday's stint,
My virtuosity of print
And grandmother's wonder:
Reading of throttler and curate,
Blood, hallelujahs and thunder,
While the generations boiled down to one
And the kettle burned dry
In a soon grandmotherless room;

Reading for forty years,
Till the print swirled out like a down-catch of soot
And the wind howled round
A world left cold and draughty,
Un-latched, un-done,
By all the little literate boys
Who hadn't been to London.

ON THE CLOSING OF MILLOM
IRONWORKS

September 1968

Wandering by the heave of the town park, wondering
Which way the day will drift,
On the spur of a habit I turn to the feathered
Weathercock of the furnace chimneys.

                                 But no grey smoke-tail
Pointers the mood of the wind. The hum
And blare that for a hundred years
Drummed at the town's deaf ears
Now fills the air with the roar of its silence.
They'll need no more to swill the slag-dust off the windows;
The curtains will be cleaner
And the grass plots greener
Round the Old Folk's council flats. The tanged autumnal mist
Is filtered free of soot and sulphur,
And the wind blows in untainted.
It's beautiful to breathe the sharp night air.
But, morning after morning, there
They stand, by the churchyard gate,
Hands in pockets, shoulders to the slag,
The men whose fathers stood there back in '28,
When their sons were at school with me.

                                 The town
Rolls round the century's bleak orbit.

                                 Down
On the ebb-tide sands, the five-funnelled
Battleship of the furnace lies beached and rusting;
Run aground, not foundered;

Not a crack in her hull;
Lacking but a loan to float her off.

The Market

Square is busy as the men file by
To sign on at the 'Brew'.[1] But not a face
Tilts upward, no-one enquires of the sky.
The smoke prognosticates no how
Or why of any practical tomorrow.
For what does it matter if it rains all day?
And what's the good of knowing
Which way the wind is blowing
When whichever way it blows it's a cold wind now.

[1] The local term for 'Bureau' – i.e. Labour Exchange – widely used
in the '30s.

NICHOLSON, SUDDENLY

From the BARROW EVENING MAIL, Thurs, 13th Feb., 1969.

'NICHOLSON—(Suddenly) on February 11,
Norman, aged 57 years, beloved husband of Mona
Nicholson, and dear father of Gerald, of 6 Atkin-
son Street, Haverigg, Millom.'

So Norman Nicholson is dead!
I saw him just three weeks ago
Standing outside a chemist's shop,
His smile alight, his cheeks aglow.
I'd never seen him looking finer:
'I can't complain at all,' he said,
'But for a touch of the old angina.'
Then hobbled in for his prescription.
Born in one town, we'd made our start,
Though not in any way related,
Two years and three streets apart,
Under one nominal description:
'Nicholson, Norman', entered, dated,
In registers of birth and school.
In 1925 we sat
At the same desk in the same class—
Me, chatty, natty, nervous, thin,
Quick for the turn of the teacher's chin;
Silent, shy and smiling, he,
And fleshed enough for two of me—
An unidentical near twin
Who never pushed his presence in
When he could keep it out.

For seven
Years after that each neither knew,
Nor cared much, where or even whether
The other lived. And then, together,
We nearly booked out berths to heaven:—
Like a church weathercock, *I* crew
A graveyard cough and went to bed
For fifteen months; *he* dropped a lead
Pipe on his foot and broke them both.
They wheeled him home to his young wife
Half-crippled for the rest of life.

In three decades or more since then
We met, perhaps, two years in ten
In shops or waiting for a bus;
Greeted each other without fuss,
Just: 'How do, Norman?'—Didn't matter
Which of us spoke—we said the same.
And now and then we'd stop to natter:
'How's the leg?' or 'How's the chest?'—
He a crock below the waist
And me a crock above it.
Blessed
Both with a certain home-bred gumption,
We stumped our way across the cobbles
Of half a life-time's bumps and roughness—
He short in step and me in wind,
Yet with a kind of wiry toughness.
Each rather sorry for the other,
We chose the road that suited best—
Neither inscribed the sky with flame;
Neither disgraced the other's name.

49

And now, perhaps, one day a year
The town will seem for half a minute
A place with one less person in it,
When I remember I'll not meet
My unlike double in the street.
Postmen will mix us up no more,
Taking my letters to his door,
For which I ought to raise a cheer.
But can I stir myself to thank
My lucky stars, when there's a blank
Where *his* stars were? For I'm left here,
Wearing his name as well as mine,
Finding the new one doesn't fit,
And, though I'll make the best of it,
Sad that such things had to be—
But glad, still, that it wasn't me.

OLD MAN AT A CRICKET MATCH

'It's mending worse,' he said,
Bending west his head,
Strands of anxiety ravelled like old rope,
Skitter of rain on the scorer's shed
His only hope.

Seven down for forty-five,
Catches like stings from a hive,
And every man on the boundary appealing—
An evening when it's bad to be alive,
And the swifts squealing.

Yet without boo or curse
He waits leg-break or hearse,
Obedient in each to law and letter—
Life and the weather mending worse,
Or worsening better.

A LOCAL PREACHER'S GOODBYE

'I'll meet you again up there'—
He pointed to the smoke
With black umbrella finger
(The chimneys tall as hymns,
Fuming with extemporary prayer)—
'I'll see you all up there,'
           He said.

Six boys or seven
In the dark October drizzle,
Class tickets in our pockets,
Ready to leave Heaven
Locked in with the hymn-books;
Supper and bed
Hard on by the Market Clock—
'Good night, Mr Fawcett, sir,'
           We said.

Forty years of soot and rain;
A Bible-insured
Ghost of chapel steward
And manufacturer of aerated waters,
With grey-ginger beard
Bubbling my unwritten poetry—
'Grand seeing you again!',
           I say.

BOND STREET

'Bond Street,' I said, 'Now where the devil's that?'—
The name of one whose face has been forgotten.—
He watched me from a proud-as-Preston hat;
His briefcase fat with business. 'See, it's written
First on my list. Don't you know your own town?'—
'Bond Street?'—Turning it over like an old coin,
Thumbing it, testing for signs.—'I copied it down
From a map in the Reading Room. In the mean-
time, I've a policy here. . . .'—Yes, on a *map*
Bond Street once looked the first of streets, more
Rakish than the Prince of Wales, the peak of the cap
Jaunted at then ungathered orchards of ore,
Damsons of haematite. Yet not a house
Was built there and the road remained unmade,
For there was none to pay the rates—a mouse
And whippet thoroughfare, engineered in mud,
Flagged with the green-slab leaves of dock and plantain,
A free run for the milk cart to turn round
From either of the two back-alleys shunted
End-on against it. But the birds soon found
Sites where the Council couldn't. From last year's broccoli
  and old
Brass bedsteads joggled in to make a fence,
Among the pigeon lofts and hen-huts, in the cold
Green-as-a-goosegog twilight, the throstles sense
That here is the one street in all the town
That no-one ever died in, that never failed
Its name or promise. The iron dust blows brown.
I turned to my enquirer.—'Bond Street I know well.

'You'll sell no insurance there.'—'I could insure
'The deaf and dumb,' he replied, 'against careless talk.'—
'Whatever you choose,' I said. 'A mile past the Square,
'Then ask again. Hope you enjoy your walk.'

TO THE MEMORY OF A MILLOM
MUSICIAN

Harry Pelleymounter,
Day by half-pay day,
Served saucepans, fire-lighters, linseed oil
Over his father's counter;
But hard on shutting-up time
He snapped the yale and stayed
Alone with the rolled linoleum
And made the shop-dusk twang.

Harry played
Saxophone, piano,
Piano-accordion
At Christmas party and Saturday hop,
While we in the after-homework dark
Rang smut-bells, sang
'Yes, yes, YES, we have no',
And clicked ink-smitted fingers
At a down-at-heel decade.

The crumbling 'Thirties
Were fumbled and riddled away;
Dirty ten bob coupons
Dropped from the pockets of war.
And Harry, dumped in the lateral
Moraine of middle-age,
Strummed back the golden dole-days
When the boys with never a chance
Went without dinner
For a tanner for the dance.

Now Harry's daughter,
Fatherless at fifteen,
Is knitting a history thesis
Of Millom in between
Her youth and Harry's:—
Statistics of gas and water
Rates, percentage of unemployed,
Standard of health enjoyed
By the bare-foot children the police ran dances
To buy boots for—and Harry played.

Pulling at threads of the dead years,
The minutes taken as read—
Spectacled, earnest, unaware
That what the Chairman left unsaid,
The print in the dried-up throat, the true
Breath of the paper bones, once blew
Through Harry's soft-hummed, tumbled tunes
She never listened to.

GREAT DAY

'I gave him an—*err*,' my father said, meaning
Masonic handshake: holding his fingers
As if they still were sticky from the royal touch.
And I, at an upstairs window (the afternoon
Raining down on the Square, the Holborn Hill Brass Bandsmen
Blowing the water out of their tubas) watched
His Royal Highness conducted through the puddles
To my father's brotherly clasp.

                    Out in the wet,
Beside the broken billboards and the derelict joiner's yard,
Two hundred primary scholars soaked and cheered,
Unseeing and unseen.

                At five o'clock that morning
We'd climbed the Jubilee Hill in the drizzling forelight
To view, in ninety-nine per cent eclipse, a sun
That never rose at all. The smoke from early fires
Seeped inconspicuously into the mist; the 5.30
Ironworks buzzer boomed out like a fog-horn. Click,
On the nick of the clock, the calculated dawn
Shied back on itself, birds knocked off shouting,
And the light went home to roost. Two minutes later
The twist of the globe turned up the dimmer
And day began again to try to begin.

                   It rained,
On and off, for eleven hours, but I
Dry in my window-seat, the sun still in eclipse,
Squinted at the prince through candle-kippered glasses,
Too young to be disappointed, too old to cheer—

Universe and dynasty poised on the tip of one parish—
Eager at last, for *God Save the King* and tea
And my father's now royally contagious hand.

THE COCK'S NEST

The spring my father died—it was winter, really,
February fill-grave, but March was in
Before we felt the bruise of it and knew
How empty the rooms were—that spring
A wren flew to our yard, over Walter Willson's
Warehouse roof and the girls' school playground
From the old allotments that are now no more than a compost
For raising dockens and cats. It found a niche
Tucked behind the pipe of the bathroom outflow,
Caged in a wickerwork of creeper; then
Began to build:
Three times a minute, hour after hour,
Backward and forward to the backyard wall,
Nipping off neb-fulls of the soot-spored moss
Rooted between the bricks. In a few days
The nest was finished. They say the cock
Leases an option of sites and leaves the hen
To choose which nest she will. She didn't choose our yard.
And as March gambolled out, the fat King-Alfred sun
Blared down too early from its tinny trumpet
On new-dug potato-beds, the still bare creeper,
The cock's nest with never an egg in,
And my father dead.

THE SEVENTEENTH OF THE NAME

When my grandmother in a carrier's cart, fording the mile and
                                        a half wide
Ebb of the Duddon, saw the black marsh sprouting
            Furnace and shack,
            'Turn the horse back!'
She cried, but the tide had turned and the horse went on. My
                            land-bred grand-
father, harnessed farm hacks to works waggons, shifted grit
                                    from the quarries,
            And laid down
            The road to the town
Before the town was there. My Uncle Bill,
Bundled in with the eggs and the luggage at fifteen months,
                            hatched out to be a blacksmith,
            Served his hour
            To horseless horse-power,
Forged shoes for machines and iron pokers, hooked
Like a butcher's skewer, for my grandmother's kitchen range.

            My Uncle Jack
            Played full-back
For the Northern Union and went in second wicket for the
                                        First Eleven.
One August Monday he smacked a six clean into an excursion
                                        train—
            'Hit it from here
            To Windermere',
My grandmother said. He broke his spine down the mine and
                            died below ground

(The family's prided loss on the iron front),
>Left, 'Not to Mourn',
>A daughter, born
After he died, and a widow who held to his memory fifty
>>years.

My Uncle Tom was a cobbler: under a crack willow of leather
>>shavings
>Tacked boot, nailed clog,
>By the twitch of dog-
eared Co-operative gas-jets in the dark of the shoe shop where
My Uncle Jim was manager. He, best-loved uncle
>And my father's friend,
>In the end
Out-lived the lot: octogenarian, in a high, stiff collar, he walked
>>his silver-
banded cane down the half-day closings
>Of a vast, life-lasting,
>Somnambulist past.
My Uncle George married Jim's wife's sister and left with my
>>Uncle Fred
To be bosses' weighman and men's check-weighman in the
>>same Durham pit. Each
>Bargained each black
>Over half tons of slack,
And they went for a walk together every Sunday morning.
My Uncle Bob, a Tom-Thumb tailor, as my grandmother
>>told me,
>Sat cross-legged all day
>On a thimble; went to stay
With George, drove out on a motor-bike and rode back in a
>>hearse.
Arnold, the youngest, hung wall-paper; Harry was a waiter;

Richard took fits. Three
Died in infancy,
Un-christened and un-sistered. One other brother
Left me what an uncle couldn't:—a face, a place, a root
That drives down deep
As St George's steeple
Heaves up high.—The church was built in the year that he was
born.—
The name is painted out on the sun-blind of my father's shop,
But yellows yet
In files of *The Millom Gazette*,
And in minutes of the Musical Festival and the Chamber of
Trade,
And in lead letters on headstones by St George's mound
It now spells out
Its what-are-you-going-to-do-about-it
Memorandum. As once when a boy I see it scratched
On backstreet slates and schoolyard gates. Step on the
gravel and the stones squeak out
'Nicholson, Nicholson.'
Whereupon
Grandmother, grandfather, father, seven known
And six clocked-out-before-me uncles stare
From their chimneyed heaven
On the seventeenth
Of the name, wondering through the holy smother where the
family's got to.
And I, in their great-grand-childless streets, rake up for my
reply
Damn all but hem
And haw about them.